Washington Crossing Historic Park

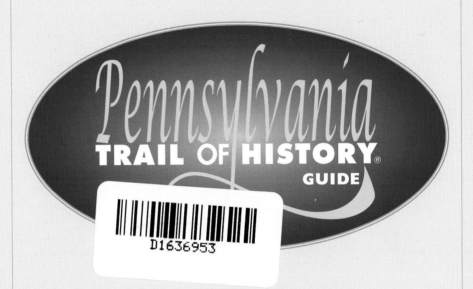

Pennsylvania TRAIL OF HISTORY® GUIDE

D1636953

Text by John Bradley
Photographs by Craig A. Benner

STACKPOLE BOOKS

PENNSYLVANIA HISTORICAL
AND MUSEUM COMMISSION

Kyle R. Weaver, Series Editor
Tracy Patterson, Designer

Published by
STACKPOLE BOOKS
5067 Ritter Road
Mechanicsburg, Pennsylvania 17055

Printed in the United States of America
2 4 6 8 10 9 7 5 3 1
FIRST EDITION

Maps by Caroline Stover

Photography
Craig A. Benner: 3, 5, 9, 11, 20, 31, 32, 35–47

Cover: Detail of *Washington Crossing the Delaware*, by Emanuel Leutze (American, born Germany, 1816–68), 1851, oil on canvas, 149 x 255 in.
THE METROPOLITAN MUSEUM OF ART, GIFT OF JOHN STEWART KENNEDY, 1897 (97.34);
PHOTOGRAPH ©1992 THE METROPOLITAN MUSEUM OF ART

Library of Congress Cataloging-in-Publication Data

Bradley, John.
    Washington Crossing Historic Park : Pennsylvania trail of history guide / text by John Bradley ; photographs by Craig A. Benner—1st ed.
        p. cm.—(Pennsylvania trail of history guides)
    Includes bibliographical references (p.).
    ISBN 0-8117-2885-4 (pbk.)
    1. Washington Crossing Historic Park (Pa.)—Guidebooks. 2. Washington, George, 1732–1799. 3. Trenton, Battle of, Trenton, N.J., 1776. 4. Delaware River Valley (N.Y.–Del. and N.J.)—History—Revolution, 1775–1783—Campaigns. 5. United States—History—Revolution, 1775–1783—Campaigns. I. Benner, Craig A. II. Pennsylvania Historical and Museum Commission. III. Title. IV. Series.

F157.B8 B56 2004
973.3'32—dc22

                                                                                    2003024615

Contents

Editor's Preface

Washington's crossing of the Delaware is one of the defining moments of the American Revolution and perhaps of American history as a whole. The victory that followed at Trenton came as an inspiration to the Continentals at a time when all hope seemed lost. Today, the moment remains important to many as a symbol of freedom, strength, and courage. The site in Pennsylvania where Washington and his troops embarked on the fateful crossing and the village that later developed around it are preserved by the Pennsylvania Historical and Museum Commission (PHMC). Stackpole Books is pleased to continue its collaboration with the PHMC to feature Washington Crossing Historic Park in this new volume of the Pennsylvania Trail of History Guides.

Each volume of the series features one of the historic sites or museums administered by the PHMC. The series was conceived and created by Stackpole Books with the cooperation of the PHMC's Division of Publications and Bureau of Historic Sites and Museums. Donna Williams heads the latter, and she and her staff of professionals review the text of each guidebook for accuracy and have made many valuable recommendations. Diane Reed, Chief of Publications, has facilitated relations between the PHMC and Stackpole from the project's inception, organized the review process with the commission, and attended to numerous details related to the venture.

The Administrator of Washington Crossing Historic Park, Michael Bertheaud, and his staff played an important part in the development of this project. Michelle Matz, Museum Educator, responded in the most professional way to a daunting list of questions. Curator Hilary Folwell Krueger made many helpful suggestions for illustrations. Craig A. Benner provided superb photographs of the site today. At Stackpole, David Reisch assisted me on production.

The author of the text, John Bradley, is a Pennsylvania historian and teacher who has previously contributed to this series with the texts for *Ephrata Cloister* and *Conrad Weiser Homestead*. In this guidebook, he provides the vital background leading up to December 25, 1776, the story of the crossing and the morale-building victories that followed, and a complete tour of the buildings and grounds of the park, which memorializes both the crossing and an early town that developed in the wake of the new nation.

Kyle R. Weaver, Editor
Stackpole Books

Introduction to the Site

Washington Crossing Historic Park is a quiet spot along the Delaware River, on the edge of the greater Philadelphia metropolitan area. The site is most prominent for a single event that took place in a span of ten hours in 1776, when a tattered, demoralized army crossed the wide, ice-filled river on its way to attack a contingent of highly disciplined professional soldiers nine miles away in Trenton. The fact that these attacking amateurs triumphed over their more skilled foes encouraged their countrymen to believe in the ultimate success of their goal. That objective, American independence, was achieved six years after the Continental Army, led by Gen. George Washington, made its precarious boat trip across the Delaware River in the winter of 1776.

Washington Crossing Historic Park represents much more than the place where Washington's Colonials launched their famous early-morning attack on the Hessians at Trenton, New Jersey. Restored Colonial buildings, such as the Thompson-Neely House and McConkey Ferry Inn, give many clues about living conditions during the Revolutionary era. Later homes and shops reveal how nineteenth-century rural Pennsylvanians lived and worked. Among them are the home of a prosperous merchant, a village general store, and homes for skilled artisans. The park also features stone memorials, picnic pavilions, and historic collections.

The Revolution in 1776

After winning the French and Indian War in 1763, Britain had a much larger empire: Canada and all of France's claims in North America were now British possessions. The wars fought by England in the colonies, at sea, and on foreign soil throughout the eighteenth century had been costly. The British government focused on taxing their subjects to pay for the empire's debt. Reasoning that the colonists were English citizens who had directly benefited from the war, the British government decided to tax them as well to help pay for it.

Over the objections of some colonists, a variety of taxes were enacted over the next several years. Among these were the Stamp Act of 1765, which taxed newspapers, legal documents, and playing cards, and the Townshend Duties of 1767, which put fees on imports such as paint, glass, and tea. Because no colonists sat in Parliament, some colonists came to feel that they were victims of "taxation without representation."

In addition, the colonists became increasingly resentful of British regulars permanently quartered in some loca-tions, such as Boston. Events such as the Boston Massacre of 1770 and a continu-ation of protests related to taxes, like the Boston Tea Party of 1773, punctuated the growing tensions between Britain and her colonies.

Punishment for the Tea Party came in the Coercive, or Intolerable, Acts, which were adopted by Parliament in the spring of 1774. These laws hammered Boston by closing the city's port to all trade, a harsh blow to a community whose econ-omy was based upon commerce. The Massachusetts Government Act banned public meetings; Boston's courts lost authority under the Administration of Justice Act; and the Quartering Act forced citizens to shelter British troops in their homes. The acts were also intended to suppress Colonial radicalism by making an example of Boston.

In response, Colonial leaders held a Continental Congress in Philadelphia to debate British treatment of the colonies and formulate responses such as boy-cotts of British goods. Although view-points varied, some colonists had come to feel that increasingly stern treatment

Independence. After Congress proclaimed its formal break with Great Britain in the Decla-ration of Independence, copies of the document were distributed around the new states and read aloud in public. LIBRARY OF CONGRESS

by Britain was eroding their rights as British citizens. Many delegates also felt that they would have to take drastic measures, including military action, to defend their rights. The thirteen colonies had little history of combined action. No political structure united them, and during wars regiments from each colony served at their own volition.

THE REVOLUTION BEGINS
On April 19, 1775, when British troops marched from Boston to Lexington and Concord to seize war supplies stored by local militias, shots were fired and the American Revolution began. The Continental Congress proclaimed that the colonies were fighting in self-defense, stating that Britain was threatening the rights and lives of its American citizens. To coordinate matters, Congress took control of the army and named Virginia's George Washington commander in chief.

Slowly Congress began to function like a national government. Improvising as it went, it tried to develop a system under which the colonies could work together. The body was weakened by its inability to tax or to require the states to contribute money or supplies. When a split developed between those who wanted reconciliation with Britain and those who thought the Colonies must become independent, Congress was further limited.

The publication of Thomas Paine's dynamic pamphlet *Common Sense* in January 1776 did much to promote the revolutionary spirit. Paine, a recent immigrant from England, wrote that monarchy was corrupt, and that Americans should break away and form a new nation based upon republican principles.

By the spring of 1776, the movement for independence had gained momentum. With some states, particularly Penn-sylvania, demonstrating reluctance to break away, Congress announced its formal separation in July 1776 with the Declaration of Independence. The document, written by Virginia's Thomas Jefferson, described the philosophical justification for revolution and listed the colonists' many grievances against Britain.

WASHINGTON'S ARMY
When Washington arrived at Boston in July 1775 to assume command of the Continental Army, he found an organization struggling with many difficulties. The army was a blend of three types of units: Continental troops who were paid by Congress, official state militia groups with close ties to their home colonies, and temporary volunteers who had come out for the immediate emergency. Those soldiers with formal enlistments had signed on for short periods of time, often as little as a year or less. Training was inadequate and military discipline was lacking. The entire army suffered from shortages of food, supplies, and weapons. Money was scarce, resulting in late pay for the men and sometimes no pay at all. As the seasons changed, men were needed at home to farm the land. In addition, an ill-clad, ill-fed army was quick to succumb to diseases, such as smallpox, malaria, and dysentery. These factors led to a high desertion rate. Throughout 1775 and 1776, the army would habitually struggle with these problems.

On the other hand, the American soldiers possessed advantages that, although intangible, gave them and their countrymen hope for victory in the battles that lay ahead. Americans felt that their virtuous citizen-soldiers had more natural courage than their professional opponents from overseas. Although most were hesitant about

Washington's Army *consisted of regular Continental troops, state militias, and volunteers.*

being soldiers, the nobleness of their cause—the preservation of American liberties—inspired them by giving them moral strength.

At the time of the Revolution, soldiers had different reasons for taking part in the cause. Some young men who were without family ties or fortunes joined for the enlistment bonuses provided by Colonial leaders. Others sought adventure, honor, and glory. Many came from various walks of life inspired by the shared vision of liberty so eloquently described by Revolutionary publicists.

Because their pay was often late in arriving, the soldiers could not purchase supplies sold at inflated prices by profiteering merchants who operated at the fringes of every encampment. Military uniforms were unavailable for many soldiers. Uniform standardization of the early war militia was difficult to address, as funds were lacking. Many men wore civilian clothes, making the appearance of the rebel army less than cohesive in comparison to their well-equipped enemy. Some men carried rifled muskets, which were more accurate than the standard flintlock smoothbore musket that most troops carried—usually either the British-made "Brown Bess" or the French "Charleyville." These smoothbore muskets could be loaded at a faster pace than the Colonial rifles. The concept used when fighting with these inaccurate weapons was to fire as many rounds as possible, thereby increasing the chances of hitting the enemy, rather than aiming for a specific target. The tactics of the time dictated that after the initial volleys, the bayonet was secured and close-rank fighting ensued. The bayonet was important to Washington's army, as supplies such as lead and powder were frequently less than adequate.

HIS MAJESTY'S TROOPS AND THE ROYAL NAVY

Opposing Washington and his troops was a British army of trained, well-equipped soldiers. In addition, thousands of auxiliary troops from German principalities, commonly known as Hessians, served with the British. The British expected that the rebellion would be subdued quickly, assuming that the ragtag colonists could never stand up to their might. But a number of factors limited the British war effort.

Believing that the Revolution had been started by a handful of radicals, the British thought that most colonists were loyal subjects who would help put down the uprising. But the help received from these loyalists did not match expectations. Britain also had long supply and communication lines, which were difficult to maintain. Its army required tons of supplies, and many ships and their crews from the Royal Navy played a key role in transporting soldiers, weapons, and baggage across the Atlantic.

The army Britain sent to America in the 1770s was Britain's largest overseas military operation in its history before the twentieth century: an unprecedented deployment of troops such a long way from home. Additionally, with international rivals such as France and Spain posing threats, the British had troops stationed at other points around the world and could not focus all of their attention on events in the rebellious Colonies.

The British were hampered by their desire to suppress the American Revolution in such a way that the colonies would come back into their place in the empire, not destroy them as they would a hated enemy. In fact, the British commanders Gen. William Howe and his brother Adm. Richard Howe held the posts of peace commissioners charged with trying to get the Americans to end their rebellion. In the dual role of warriors and peacemakers, the Howes may not have wanted to wage the all-out kind of war they would have fought against a foreign foe.

NEW YORK: WHERE THE STORY OF WASHINGTON CROSSING REALLY BEGINS

In March 1776, the occupying British Army boarded a fleet of ships and left Boston. Any comfort the Americans may have felt from this move was tempered by the realization that the English were likely to strike elsewhere. In Washington's mind, New York was the likely spot, and he immediately began to plan the city's defense. The commander's prediction came true in June, when twenty-five thousand British troops landed on Staten Island. Among their ranks were proud regiments of Hessian fighters ready to make short work of their amateur opponents.

In the summer and fall of 1776, the Continental Army stumbled through a disastrous series of battles in the New York City area, losing encounters in Brooklyn and Manhattan, and on the mainland north of the city. The string of defeats led some colonists to question Washington's leadership and to wonder if his army had even the slimmest chance for a victory.

More than once, miraculous escapes saved Washington's army from total destruction. When his army was pinned against the East River on Long Island, only the dramatic intervention of a seagoing unit from Massachusetts known as the Marblehead Mariners rescued the beleaguered forces. The Marbleheaders' splendid amphibious effort of August 29 and 30, which saved approximately nine thousand men and their equipment, was one of the most dramatic troop movements of the entire war. Led by their spirited commander, John Glover, the Mariners prevented the Americans from being trapped on Manhattan in mid-September, and one month later they fought valiantly in the Battle of Harlem Heights. In fact, if there was anything positive arising from the New York campaign, it proved to Washington that the waterways were a tool he could use to the army's advantage.

After the British and their Hessian allies overwhelmed Forts Washington and Lee overlooking the Hudson River, one patriot wrote the dismal phrase "a shudder went thro' the continent." It was now mid-November, and the situation

The British Army, highly trained and well-equipped, contrasted starkly with the motley Continentals.

HESSIAN MERCENARIES
OR GERMAN AUXILIARIES?

During the era of the American Revolution, more than three hundred city-states, some quite tiny, occupied the land we now know as Germany. And more than thirty thousand soldiers from the German city-states fought for Britain during the American struggle for independence, including the three regiments surprised by Washington's men on the morning after the crossing.

Britain, whose crown was related to the Austrian and Prussian empires by family ties, paid six German rulers for the services of professional military units in its American war. Thus the British received additional battle-hardened regiments, while the Germans expected to gain practical experience for their soldiers and officers.

A *mercenary*, as we use the term today, is an individual who voluntarily serves in a foreign army for pay. When entire regiments are shipped by one country to another, it may be more precise to apply the term *auxiliaries*.

Strictly speaking, not all of the thirty thousand German auxiliaries who fought against the Continentals should be called Hessians. A prominent region of central-western Germany, Hesse, itself fractured into subregions, was only one of the many sections of that country before its unification. The largest contingent of German fighters contracted to the British came from Hesse-Cassel, whose prince, Frederick II, supplied twelve thousand men. The three regiments surprised at Trenton after Washington's crossing came from this region; they and men from nearby Hesse-Hanau were true "Hessians."

Fusiliers and grenadiers, the Hessians were widely considered to be among the finest soldiers of Europe. Their fierce reputation was enhanced by their successes in the New York Campaign, but the Hessians began to lose some of their mystique after Trenton showed that they were not invincible. Indeed, original writings reveal that some Germans came to fear the Americans, with their unconventional fighting styles and frontiersman reputations,

Hessian Soldiers served the British crown but wore their own unique uniforms. LIBRARY OF CONGRESS

nearly as much as the rebels dreaded seeing the tall brass miter cap through the smoke of battle.

Four other German city-states also supplied men to England during the Revolution. They were Anhalt-Zerbst, Ansbach-Bayreuth, Brunswick, and Waldeck. The thirty thousand Hessians who eventually served with the British in the American Revolution made up one-third of the total number of British forces. In most cases, the Hessians remained in segregated regiments, serving under their own commanders, following their own flags, and wearing their own distinctive uniforms. Communication between British and Hessian units was not always easy, as many of the top British commanders, including General Howe, did not speak German.

Hessian troops fought intensely in the battles around New York City, especially in the capture of the American stronghold known as Fort Washington, where they overwhelmed the defenders, appearing invincible in a charge where bugles blared and pointed bayonets slashed. Many British subjects felt dismayed that their government had hired foreign troops to use against their own people. Some saw the Hessians as hired assassins who had come to destroy the Colonists. One of the sharpest grievances in the Declaration of Independence condemned the "foreign mercenaries" brought to America who were guilty of "cruelty and perfidy" while carrying out their "works of death, desolation, & tyranny." The Hessians did not help their reputation by pillaging food and supplies from both loyalists and patriots. Reports of crimes against property and brutal behavior toward civilians strengthened American hatred of these foreign professional troops.

After the Revolution, only seventeen thousand of the auxiliaries returned to Germany. Roughly seventy-five hundred had died in battle or from illness, and the remaining five thousand had been captured, deserted, or simply chose to stay in America at war's end.

looked grim for the revolution's survival. With a dwindling army, an aggressive foe, and questionable generalship, how could the revolutionaries hope to prevail?

Having lost 3,000 men killed, wounded, deserted, or taken prisoner, 2,800 muskets, and 150 cannons in the losses of Forts Washington and Lee, the Continentals retreated to northern New Jersey with the confident enemy in pursuit. After seeing how the Hessian regiments had fought ferociously around New York, the Continental Army had come to both fear and hate these foreign auxiliaries. Washington had to preserve his army and was unwilling to risk the casualties of a major battle. Begrudgingly he gave ground, moving south and west, managing to stay just ahead of the pursuing British. Washington expected reinforcements to aid his retreat. One hopeful thought may have lingered in the commander's mind: Although he currently could not outfight the British and Hessians in a pitched battle, the nautical skills of the Marblehead Mariners would allow him to outmaneuver the enemy on waterways. Large rivers and waterways would also serve as a barrier between the armies, allowing Washington time to regroup. That mobility, and the very size of the territory he was fighting to defend, would be Washington's two assets in this time of crisis.

Washington called for assistance from the New Jersey militia but was disappointed when little help came. Keenly divided between patriots and loyalists, New Jersey was decidedly unenthusiastic in its support of the revolution. This ambivalent attitude toward rebellion was hardly unique, for throughout the colonies the politics of revolution were complicated by many internal issues.

Even in New Jersey, which was reputed to have the best road system in the colonies, overland travel was slow. More mobile than their foe, who had to carry with them a large amount of supplies and food, the Americans kept out of reach as they plodded over the muddy roads and crossed the rivers on narrow bridges. As the pursuit entered central New Jersey, Washington grew concerned that the British were aiming toward Philadelphia, seat of Congress and the capital of the United States. Though the American retreat across New Jersey was orderly, the continual falling back discouraged everyone, including the commander, who, in a letter to his brother back home in Virginia, gloomily predicted: "The game will be pretty well up."

The pursuing army of British and Hessians proceeded cautiously, concerned about stumbling into a trap. The deliberate pace of the British was surprising to some, including many local loyalists, who thought that a quick strike against the remnants of the rebel force could end the revolution then and there. But the troops were relentless, forcing Washington to keep on the move. Some British and Hessians plundered homes and farms along their route, not bothering to distinguish between loyalists and patriots. This thievery did not help the British cause among the local citizens, even though some Continental soldiers committed the same offense.

Traveling through New Brunswick, Princeton, and into southwestern New Jersey, Washington began to plan his next move. Looking farther west, he realized that the Delaware River, which divided New Jersey and Pennsylvania, would be an excellent defensive barrier for his army and a block to the British advance.

As he approached the river, Washington sent orders ahead for all boats to be

Charles, Lord Cornwallis, commanded the British troops that pursued Washington through New Jersey. NATIONAL PORTRAIT GALLERY, LONDON

secured between Easton and Philadelphia. Craft needed to move his army across the river were taken to one location, and all remaining boats were moved to the Pennsylvania side or destroyed. Because of its width, the Delaware had no bridges at the time of the Revolution. It could be crossed only by boat.

Washington arrived at Trenton, a village on the banks of the Delaware, in early December. Sending his army's minimal gear and supplies across the river to Pennsylvania, he remained on the New Jersey side briefly before ordering his men to cross ahead of the arrival of the British advance forces, commanded by Lord Charles Cornwallis. Once again those intrepid Massachusetts seamen and fishermen, the Marbleheaders, came to the rescue, ferrying the troops across the wide river safely. Washington's army started its crossing on December 7 and finished the next day.

THE REVOLUTION COMES TO PENNSYLVANIA

On their first night in Pennsylvania, the men slept out in the cold open air. As one soldier later described it, "We lay amongst the leaves without tents or blankets, laying down with our feet to the fire." Eventually most of the enlisted men were sheltered in barns, mills, or other structures. Most of the men lacked decent shoes and warm clothes, as many of their supplies had been captured by the British during the losses of Forts Washington and Lee. What clothes the men did have with them were wearing thin as they retreated across New Jersey in the cooler temperatures of late fall. The artist Charles Willson Peale, who had come to help the cause in early December, referred to the army as "half-naked veterans of the long retreat."

Many of the higher-ranking officers set up headquarters in homes in Bucks County. Close enough for easy travel among them, these buildings became the meeting places of the generals, including John Sullivan, Nathanael Greene, Henry Knox, and William Stirling, who advised Washington on the conduct of the war. Bowman's Hill also gave the Americans a valuable watch point; community lore tells of scouts at its summit looking up and down the river for miles, scanning vigilantly to see if the enemy was attempting a crossing.

Washington's first Pennsylvania headquarters was at Morrisville, a village across the river from Trenton, in the southern portion of Bucks County. By December 13, he moved to a more central location, the Keith House in Upper Makefield Township, close to the McConkey Ferry Inn, so he could better communicate with his troops.

For the next three weeks, Washington's army remained temporarily encamped on the Pennsylvania side of the Delaware River. With his troops relatively secure, Washington could now take steps to preserve his army and restore the revolution from his new headquarters.

The army was now spread out along the river, concentrated at points where ferries could cross, watching vigilantly for British activity. Washington ordered his troops to build earth and wooden fortifications known as redoubts at ferry landings and other likely crossing points. At times the men went out foraging, confiscating supplies from the local citizens, although Washington tried to curtail this because of the ill will it generated among the civilians.

Despite being both emotionally and physically exhausted by his retreat across New Jersey, Washington could not enjoy the peace and quiet of a Bucks County winter. Unlike his adversary, General Howe, who was able to take advantage of the New York social scene, Washington had many responsibilities to fulfill in order to preserve his army and sustain the revolution. Most immediate was the task of preventing the remaining British units from crossing over to the Pennsylvania side of the Delaware. This meant keeping his troops alert to any signs of British attempts to build boats, rafts, or pontoon bridges.

Though Washington was not able to get a precise count of his troops, he knew the numbers were dwindling rapidly. With the increasing number of daily desertions, loss of men captured, and those unfit to fight due to illness, Washington's army by December 1776 had dropped to an estimated three thousand able-bodied men. Because the soldiers had not been paid in some time, most of them were expected to leave the army as soon as they were able. And many men's terms of enlistment would expire on December 31, leaving Washington with a scant number of troops.

THE BRITISH RETURN TO NEW YORK

Meanwhile, the bulk of the British forces returned to New York, where they went into winter quarters, awaiting supplies and planning for spring and the beginning of the next combat season. They left behind small groups of soldiers to man outposts in towns across New Jersey, including New Brunswick, Princeton, and Trenton. In some cases, such as Trenton, these troops found shelter in barracks that had been built nearly twenty years earlier during the French and Indian War. These defensive positions were manned mainly by Hessian troops who had fought well in the battles around New York earlier in the year. The garrison at Trenton was made up of three regiments of Hessian soldiers.

Although Howe knew that the isolated outposts were possibly vulnerable to surprise attacks, by this time he had so little regard for the Colonists that he had no fear of their army mounting any kind of assault. The Hessians shared Howe's opinion of their American rivals, believing these country farmers were no match for the highly trained and disciplined soldiers from Europe. About the only problem the Hessian outposts faced was occasional nighttime raids by tiny groups of rebels whose hit-and-run tactics were difficult to defend against. But these assaults were of little concern to the British.

Howe undoubtedly felt secure in the knowledge that he had driven the enemy into Pennsylvania, where the weakened rebels would pose no threat to his base. He knew that many of Washington's men were approaching the end of their terms of enlistment. Many colonists, among them Richard Stockton, a signer of the Declaration of Independence, believing the rebellion faced certain defeat, took advantage of Howe's offer of amnesty in return for signing an oath of loyalty to the king.

WASHINGTON AT TRENTON

Despite his lack of formal military training, which made him suspect in the eyes of both the enemy and many of his countrymen, George Washington had learned on the job a number of skills

Washington's Subordinates, clockwise from top left, John Sullivan, Nathanael Greene, William Alexander (Lord Stirling), and Henry Knox. This quartet of officers advised Washington throughout the campaign. Sullivan and Greene commanded divisions, while Alexander headed a brigade and Knox led the artillery. INDEPENDENCE NATIONAL HISTORICAL PARK

that enabled him to survive as commander of the ragtag Continental Army. Among these was flexibility—the ability to react to situations in unexpected ways and to improvise when needed, since formal maneuvering and tactics were not possible. Washington knew that he could not hope to defeat the British in the open field. He would have to employ other, highly unconventional forms of engagement to harry the opponent and buy time for his suffering army.

Only an unusual action, a tactic completely unexpected by the enemy, could end the Continentals' string of crippling defeats in 1776 and restore hope for the achievement of liberty. Drawing upon the experiences of his army's encounters, escapes, and retreats dating back to the New York Campaign, Washington began to strategize about a positive, decisive action to stem the tide.

A bold move coming in winter would achieve a number of results. First, a victorious strike at the enemy would boost the morale of the army and encourage the men to continue while also attracting new recruits. Second, the entire country would benefit from a victory, large or small, as evidence that the British and Hessian forces were not invincible and that the revolution could succeed. Third, a victory on the battlefield might persuade a skeptical Congress to approve additional, desperately needed funding for the war effort. Finally, if Washington could counterstrike with success, he could justify and solidify his command of the revolutionary forces.

Reports from New Jersey had informed Washington of the departure of the main British force for New York and the exact locations of the dispersed outposts of Hessian auxiliary forces. He decided to focus on the Hessian encampment in and around Trenton, a small village at the Falls of the Delaware, the northernmost point on the river to which oceangoing ships could travel. Additionally, several important roads converged here, making it a frequent stopping place for travelers journeying from New York and New England to Philadelphia, Maryland, and the South.

While Washington and his advisors mulled over plans for a strategic strike against the Hessians, his soldiers were kept busy drilling and preparing for battle. According to tradition, the men were read an inspirational essay written by Thomas Paine, author of *Common Sense*, which had encouraged many Colonists to favor independence a year earlier. Reacting to the battlefield disasters of the New York Campaign, Paine used the flat surface of a drumhead as his writing board while he accompanied the troops on their march across New Jersey. *The American Crisis* was published in a Philadelphia newspaper on December 19. "These are the times that try men's souls," Paine began. "The summer soldier and the sunshine patriot will in this crisis shrink from the service of their country, but he that stands it now deserves the love and thanks of man and woman." With these powerful words, simply and elegantly stated, Paine inspired men to stand firm in this time of extreme hardship.

Washington's Crossing and the Ten Crucial Days

Between December 25, 1776, and January 3, 1777, known as the "Ten Crucial Days," George Washington's army achieved several successes that altered the course of the Revolution. From its lowest point, when the struggle for freedom appeared all but lost, the triumphs of these ten days revitalized the people, their army, and their fighting spirit.

While concocting his audacious plan to mount an offensive against the enemy, Washington drew upon the counsel and experience of several of his key subordinate officers. Among them was twenty-six-year-old Henry Knox, a former bookseller from Boston who was well read in military strategy and commanded the American artillery. Other New Englanders in Washington's circle of advisors were John Sullivan, a capable general from New Hampshire, and Nathanael Greene, an ironmaker from Rhode Island, who impressed Washington with his masterful organizational ability.

Then there was William Alexander, a wealthy merchant from the Jerseys who claimed the Scottish title of earl of Stirling. An aggressive fighter and general, Lord Stirling had recently been released from British capture. Not as fortunate was Gen. Charles Lee, taken prisoner by a British patrol led by Cornet Banastre Tarleton in Basking Ridge, New Jersey. Lee had left his troops to visit Mrs. White's tavern, where he was found and captured. At the time, he was slowly and reluctantly moving his troops toward Washington's main force in Bucks County. Washington had pleaded with Lee to bring his troops quickly to his aid. Lee, however, was not inclined to accommodate the general, as he felt Washington was unfit to lead. A former British officer who had served in many foreign campaigns, Lee was contemptuous of Washington, wanting command of the American force for himself. The removal of Lee proved to be fortuitous for Washington, who was finally able to command this section of the army without a popular subordinate questioning his every move. Lee's second in command, Sullivan, quickly brought the troops to join Washington's contingent.

George Washington at Princeton. *American victories in the New Jersey Campaign transformed Washington into a national hero. Charles Willson Peale later painted the triumphant general in 1779.* U.S. SENATE COLLECTION

19

TAVERN LIFE

In Colonial days, community residents and travelers alike patronized taverns. Found in many locations—town centers, near bridges and ferries, and at backcountry crossroads— taverns provided travelers with shelter, warmth, food and drink, and overnight lodging. Taverns also were places where local folks could catch up on community gossip, read the newspaper, and obtain their mail, delivered here by the provincial postal system.

Some busy routes, such as Pennsylvania's Lancaster Turnpike, featured a tavern almost every mile, while on other stretches they were situated farther apart. The McConkey Ferry Inn, a prominent feature of Washington Crossing Historic Park, is a prime example of a riverside tavern located both on a major thoroughfare and at a crossing point of a major river. Thus it was ideally suited to take advantage of the daily traffic, whether local commercial travelers or long-distance voyagers headed through New Jersey to New York and New England. For the Philadelphia-bound, the inn marked the near end of the journey; for those heading to the tobacco plantations of the South, it was just another stop on a long trip.

According to historian Stephanie Grauman Wolf, taverns were the most numerous of all Colonial business enterprises. Lawmakers regulated the granting of licenses; restricted sales to certain groups, such as women, Native Americans, African Americans, and apprentices; and attempted to place controls on prices.

Most taverns offered overnight accommodations, although quality was uneven and the availability of clean sheets and privacy could not be taken for granted. Food of varying palatability was available, as were a wide range of alcoholic beverages, including beer, cider, rum converted from West Indies sugar and molasses, and jugs of powerful corn whiskey. The list of wines included varieties made from grapes, cherries, elderberries, flowers such as dandelion and goldenrod, and mead, made from honey.

McConkey Ferry Inn. Taverns were an important part of colonial life. Travelers stopped at these roadside havens to rest from the road, imbibe spirits, and trade gossip. Legend holds that before the crossing George Washington dined at the tavern owned by Samuel McConkey.

The campaign began on Christmas afternoon, December 25, 1776, when Washington's orders set in motion a three-pronged attack on the Hessian outposts in and around Trenton, intended to reach the village before the following dawn. An early-morning surprise attack would catch the enemy off guard, preventing them from getting into their formal battle formation in which they fought so lethally. One unit of more than five hundred militia from Pennsylvania and New Jersey, under Brig. Gen. James Ewing, was assigned to cross the Delaware at Trenton Ferry. To the south, at Bristol, a second unit of nineteen hundred soldiers, led by Lt. Col. John Cadwalader, would attack a Hessian regiment at Bordentown and block any southern escape by the Trenton forces. Washington and the main body of troops would cross the river at McConkey Ferry, then march nine miles south to Trenton to begin the attack on the unsuspecting enemy.

The men were ordered to "parade with their arms, accouterments and ammunition, in the best order, with their provisions and blankets." Each carrying three days' rations and forty rounds of ammunition, the troops marched toward the river in eerie silence. The password given to this secret mission was "Victory or Death." The men had been warned that any soldier who broke away from his unit would be shot. This was a serious undertaking, indeed.

THE CHRISTMAS CROSSING

Under the darkening sky, sometime after 4 P.M., the crossing at McConkey Ferry began. With the temperature already near freezing, the boatmen of the Marblehead Mariner regiment, under Colonel Glover, had the task of

CHRONOLOGY

March 1776 The British leave Boston; Washington prepares a defense of New York

June 25 Twenty-five thousand British and Hessian troops land at Staten Island, New York

July 4 Congress issues the Declaration of Independence

August 26–27 The British defeat the Continentals in the Battle of Long Island

September 15 The British defeat the Continentals in Manhattan and at Harlem Heights

October 28 The British defeat the Continentals in the Battle of White Plains

November 15 The British capture Fort Washington, on the Hudson River, in Manhattan

November 20 The British capture Fort Lee, on the Hudson, in New Jersey

November 22 Washington begins to move his troops across New Jersey, followed by the British

December 3 The Americans arrive at the Delaware River and move their gear and supplies across to Bucks County

(continued)

transporting twenty-four hundred men, eighteen artillery pieces, fifty to seventy-five horses, and other supplies to the Trenton side of the Delaware River. The cannons were cumbersome to move, but their firepower would give the Americans a decided edge once the battle began.

Snow and sleet fell as the troops boarded their vessels and the temperature continued to plummet. With the river at flood stage, the swift current carried large chunks of ice that had to be avoided, and the harsh wind threatened to blow the vessels off course.

As the boats arrived on the New Jersey shore, local patriots helped steady the craft and assisted the disembarking men, while others kept an eye out for British spies. Washington had forbade fires, so the men shivered in the frigid dark, pelted by the sharp bits of sleet. The exact time when Washington himself crossed is unknown. Some sources say

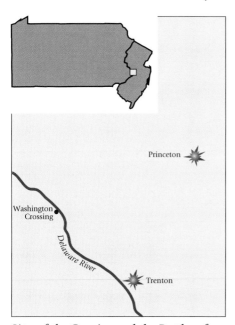

Sites of the Crossing and the Battles of Trenton and Princeton.

he traveled in one of the first boats and remained on the Jersey side while Knox and Glover coordinated the subsequent crossings of the icy river. Other sources say he stood at the McConkey Ferry Inn and watched the crossings from there. When all of the men and materiel had crossed safely, the expedition set out for Trenton.

Washington had no way of knowing that his was the only part of the three-pronged attack that had made it across the river and was going ahead with the plan devised so carefully. The forces assigned to cross the river at Trenton Ferry and at Bristol had both abandoned the assault. Ewing's Pennsylvania and New Jersey militiamen did not attempt to cross due to the strong current and ice floes. Cadwalader's infantrymen did make it to New Jersey but returned to Bucks County because they were unable to ferry their cannons across. And both commanders assumed that Washington had surely called off his part of the plan. With no communication between them, each force had to act independently. Although Washington did not know that his two subsidiary units were not participating in the attack, neither did the Hessians know that a force twice the size of their garrison was on its way toward their camp.

The crossing had taken longer than Washington had planned. It was nearly 4 A.M. on the twenty-sixth when the Continental Army began its single-file march, the units staying together, enlisted men following their officers toward their unsuspecting objective.

About 6 A.M., Washington paused near the outskirts of Trenton and split his forces once again, sending half of the army, led by Maj. Gen. Nathanael Greene, straight down Pennington Road to the enemy stronghold. The other half, under the command of Maj. Gen. John Sullivan, was ordered to circle to the east, closer to the river, and strike the west side of Trenton at the same time that the first unit attacked from the north. This plan was risky because once the flanking force was out of sight, Washington would not know its location or whether it would arrive at its objective at the proper moment.

THE HESSIANS AT TRENTON

Col. Johann Rall (also spelled Rahl or Raul), a career soldier who had entered military service at age fourteen, commanded the fifteen hundred Hessians stationed at Trenton. Now fifty, he had fought so vigorously at Fort Washington that he had been nicknamed the "Hessian Lion" by the British officers. His command at Trenton had come as a reward for his bravery and leadership in the New York campaign. But Rall, known for his aggressiveness, did not always exercise the best judgment.

Because of his contempt for the American forces, whom he dismissed as "clowns," Rall did not execute the orders he had received to construct defensive emplacements known as redoubts around Trenton, considering them unnecessary and a waste of time and effort. "Let them come," he exclaimed. "We want no trenches! We'll at them with the bayonet!" Rall also did not follow through with plans to send out mobile patrols to check the neighborhood for rebel actions: spies, raiding parties, or other groups intent on harassing his forces.

But the Hessian Lion was not entirely careless: He kept one regiment on duty at all times, fully dressed and ready to spring into combat at a moment's notice. He also informed his superiors that he felt his garrison was stretched too thin.

CHRONOLOGY

December 7 The American troops cross the river and encamp in Bucks County

December 13 Howe goes into winter quarters in New York City

December 14 Col. Johann Rall takes command of the Hessian outpost in Trenton, New Jersey

December 23 Washington tells his generals of his plan to attack Trenton; the first pamphlet in Thomas Paine's series The Crisis is published

December 25 At sundown, American troops begin to cross the Delaware River

December 26 The troops march on Trenton, open fire, and win the Battle of Trenton; then the victors return to Pennsylvania with their prisoners

December 28 Washington leads his army back to Trenton

January 2, 1777 Lord Cornwallis's British troops attack the Americans in the Second Battle of Trenton

January 3 The Americans slip out of Trenton and move toward Princeton; they are victorious in the Battle of Princeton; they then move on to Morristown, New Jersey, to set up winter quarters

Like other officers of his rank and class, Rall enjoyed fine food, drinks, and military band music. On Christmas night, he stayed up late socializing, and he was still asleep when Washington attacked the next morning. Contrary to popular belief, there is no evidence that the Hessians were intoxicated on the morning of December 26. They may have celebrated the Christmas holiday with food, spirits, and singing, but alcohol was a customary part of all soldiers' rations at the time, provided in quantities that would not produce intoxication.

THE BATTLE OF TRENTON AND ITS AFTERMATH

Washington's plan had been to catch Rall's men before dawn, while they were still asleep, using the cover of darkness to shield his approach. But because the crossing had taken so long, the attack on

Trenton did not begin until about 8 A.M., when American cannoneers began to fire on the town from a high spot north of the village where King and Queen Streets converged. (The Trenton Battle monument is located there today.) The artillery was loaded with grapeshot, clusters of iron balls that were especially lethal against unprotected troops. Because the rain and sleet did not hamper the operation of the cannons, they could fire at their usual rate of one to two rounds per minute.

As the first blue-coated Hessians stumbled out into the street to repel what they assumed was just another raiding party, they were astonished to see a large American force assembled before them. Soon the air was filled with cries of "Der Feind! Heraus!" ("The enemy! Fall out!"). The sleet that had pelted the troops on their long

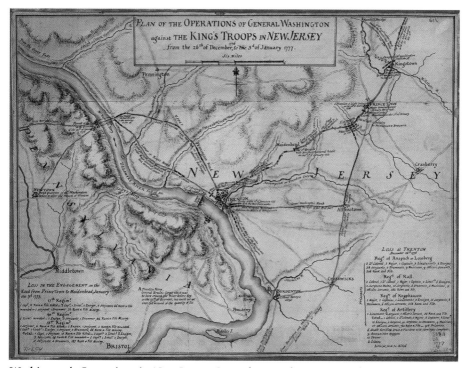

Washington's Operations in New Jersey. *Created in London in 1777, the map shows the disposition of American and British forces during the campaign.* LIBRARY OF CONGRESS

The Capture of the Hessians at Trenton, 26 December 1776. *The surprised Hessians were unable to mount effective resistance to the American assault, and nearly one thousand fell prisoner to the Continental army. John Trumbull depicted the scene in 1786.*

march to Trenton now worked in their favor, for it blew against their backs but right into the eyes and faces of the Hessians. According to tradition, the Americans had kept their muskets under cover and thus had dry gunpowder, but many of the Hessians could not get their wet weapons to respond. The confusion kept the Hessians from getting into their practiced battle formations, and thus they were not able to mount an effective defense using the tactics in which they were trained.

The second prong of the attack reached Trenton at precisely the right time and added to the success of Washington's plan. However, as the Hessians retreated to the south side of town, there was no force there to stop them, as Ewing had not crossed, and about one-third were able to slip away, avoiding what would have been a total dis-

aster. After two hours of fighting, with Colonel Rall severely wounded, the remaining Hessians surrendered the town and were taken prisoner. An exultant Washington called the victory "a glorious day for our country."

Jubilant soldiers found the town's supply of forty gallons of rum and partook of the beverage before Washington ordered its destruction. Considering a move toward another Hessian outpost, Washington and his officers agreed not to compromise the day's victory by pushing the troops beyond their physical limits. The army began the return to Pennsylvania with more than 980 Hessian prisoners, including a complete military band and its instruments. More important, they acquired food, clothing, more than one thousand muskets, six brass cannons, and other desperately needed supplies. And, significantly,

William Washington, kin to the commander in chief, was among the wounded at Trenton. He later distinguished himself in the war's southern theater and sat for this Charles Willson Peale portrait circa 1783.
INDEPENDENCE NATIONAL HISTORICAL PARK

central Pennsylvania, including towns such as Lancaster, where a stockade to house them had been constructed. Skilled craftsmen among the Hessians were soon sent to work at their trades, and the others were assigned to farmers in the region as laborers. According to tradition, Colonel Rall, who died of his wounds from the battle, was buried in Trenton in the corner of the Presbyterian cemetery.

The victory at Trenton achieved part of Washington's goal by reversing months of losses at a time when such a victory was desperately needed. It also demonstrated the prowess of his army in being able to defeat a unit of a highly acclaimed professional army. Placed in context, the Battle of Trenton may have been a skirmish, won because of propitious timing, and difficult weather conditions. But it was no small victory, as it reinvigorated the revolutionary cause and demonstrated to potential European allies, including France, that all was not lost.

However, Washington was now faced with another challenge: the problem of holding his army together before the end of December. Once again he used a brilliant strategy. On December 28, the American army crossed the Delaware back into New Jersey, returning to Trenton, the site of their recent victory, now covered with six inches of newly fallen snow. With Trenton as the backdrop for his pleas, Washington spoke to each regiment, asking the men to extend their enlistment by an additional six weeks. He promised each man who would do this a cash bonus of $10, although he had no idea where the money would come from.

To his request for six more weeks of service, there was no response. In this tense moment, silence meant a firm no.

there was no documented loss of life on the American side. Two notable men, however, were wounded during the engagement—a young James Monroe, later to become the fifth President of the United States, and George Washington's cousin, William Washington. These men were brought to the temporary military hospital at the Thompson-Neely House to convalesce.

In keeping with practices of the era, some of the captured Hessian officers were kept in the McConkey Ferry Inn while the enlisted men stayed in more primitive quarters elsewhere in the region. Subsequently, many of the prisoners were marched south to Philadelphia, where they were exhibited to the crowds in a parade through the city streets before the officers were moved south. The enlisted men were sent to

Desperate now, Washington asked the men for one more month, again with the $10 bonus. Finally a total of twelve hundred men agreed to remain, and thirty-four hundred militia joined them as well. Soon a parcel arrived from congressional treasurer Robert Morris, the principal financier of the Revolution. Morris had scraped together $50,000, some of it in paper money for paying the troops, the remainder in coins to pay informers and spies who could give information about the British actions in New Jersey.

THE SECOND BATTLE OF TRENTON AND THE BATTLE OF PRINCETON

The Trenton victory did not invigorate just the Americans. Back in New York, Gen. Charles Cornwallis abruptly canceled his plans to sail home to England. Cornwallis, who had nearly caught Washington in the Americans' march across New Jersey, now organized an eight-thousand-man army of British and Hessians and began an overland trek to Trenton on New Year's Day. The determined Cornwallis intended to avenge the Battle of Trenton by crushing Washington's army.

Cornwallis's speedy march toward Trenton went smoothly until he ran into units, such as Col. Edward Hand's Pennsylvania riflemen, outside Trenton on January 2. Crack shots, these frontiersmen unleashed a lethal barrage from their precise weapons, breaking the momentum of the advance as they picked off enemy targets. The Pennsylvania riflemen made a major contribution by harrassing and delaying Cornwallis long enough that he could not enter Trenton until late in the day.

The British followed the riflemen and pickets as they slowly gave ground and ran toward Washington's entrenched army, which secured the high ground around the Assunpink Creek. The bridge crossing the creek became a scene of intense fighting as Cornwallis's British troops and Hessian contingents struggled to capture Washington's army during this Second Battle of Trenton, also known as the Battle of the Assunpink. As the British attempted to advance and cross the bridge, the Continentals fired upon them until, as one observer noted, "the bridge looked red as blood, with their killed and wounded and their red

Plan of Princeton. On December 31, 1776, American Col. John Cadwalader scouted the British positions at Princeton and sketched this map for General Washington.
LIBRARY OF CONGRESS

APPRECIATING
WASHINGTON CROSSING THE DELAWARE

In its Visitor Center, Washington Crossing Historic Park displays an exact photo reproduction of one of America's most famous paintings, *Washington Crossing the Delaware*, by Emanuel Leutze. This digitally mastered duplicate, at twenty-one by twelve feet, is the same size as the work that hangs in New York's Metropolitan Museum of Art. Completed in 1851, the work was created in Dusseldorf, Germany, then a vibrant art center that promoted historical painting.

Sharp-eyed critics can have fun finding fault with Leutze's depiction of the events of Christmas Day 1776. The Stars and Stripes flag had not been designed yet. The crossing took place at night, so why is there so much light in the picture? The miniature icebergs flowing down the Delaware are greatly exaggerated. Finally, would Washington, or anyone else for that matter, have been standing upright in a shallow boat during a difficult river crossing?

But viewing the work in this manner misses the point Leutze intended. The painting must be seen and interpreted in the context in which it was created. Though the artist grew up in the United States, he was born in Germany and returned to his homeland for formal instruction. At the time he created *Washington Crossing the Delaware*, Leutze was working in preunification Germany, where many people were excited about democracy and personal freedoms. But an attempt to install democratic features like those flourishing in America into the German system failed in 1848, disappointing many writers, artists, and other creative people, Leutze among them. Later Leutze came back to America, where he was celebrated for his depictions of our country's historical themes, such as his masterful mural *Westward the Course of Empire Takes Its Way* displayed in the U.S. Capitol.

Washington Crossing the Delaware expresses Leutze's admiration for Washington's triumph at Trenton and the success of the American Revolution. Strength, bravery, courage, idealism, and many other virtues are reflected in the painting. If seeing it inspires the individual viewer to emulate these qualities, or reminds a nation of the importance of democracy, liberty, and personal freedoms, then it has accomplished what the artist intended.

On another level, we may also celebrate *Washington Crossing the Delaware* as an essential enduring image, or icon, of American culture. Taking its place among works known to all of us, Leutze's painting is indelibly etched

coats." The British losses were so high that they have never been enumerated precisely.

American casualties were also high, as the British and Hessian artillerists continued to level their cannons into the direct line of the troops at a fairly close range. As darkness fell, Cornwallis decided to halt the advances for the evening, confident that his superior forces would win a victory the next day with Washington's troops pinned between the creek and the Delaware River. Likening the situation to an aristocratic sport of his homeland, Cornwallis was reported to have said that he would "bag the fox" in the morning.

Washington, realizing he could not hold back the force much longer, decided to abandon Trenton and use the cover of darkness to move his army on to Princeton. Once again Cornwallis was denied a chance to capture his enemy: The "fox" was gone.

As they moved toward a small British detachment stationed in Princeton, the American troops ran into an enemy force moving south toward Trenton.

Washington Crossing the Delaware. *The oil on canvas scene (149" x 255") was painted by Emanuel Leutze (American, born Germany, 1816–68) in 1851.* THE METROPOLITAN MUSEUM OF ART, GIFT OF JOHN STEWART KENNEDY, 1897 (97.34) PHOTOGRAPH ©1992 THE METROPOLITAN MUSEUM OF ART

into our social history as much as a Gilbert Stuart portrait of George Washington, James Abbott McNeill Whistler's painting of his mother in her Quaker grays and blacks, and the dour, pitchfork-toting midwestern man and woman in Grant Wood's *American Gothic*. And for wartime bravery and devotion to the cause, can there be any doubt that *Washington Crossing the Delaware* is no less majestic than Joe Rosenthal's 1945 photograph of members of the 5th Marine Division planting the Stars and Stripes on Iwo Jima?

Fierce fighting broke out, with the British getting the better of the Colonists. Then Washington, accompanied by a mounted unit from Philadelphia, the 1st City Cavalry, took direct charge of the fighting. He plunged into action, vigorously leading an assault, and at one point found himself out in the open between the opposing lines as a volley of musket fire went off. When the smoke cleared, the commander was untouched.

The rebel forces continued on to Princeton, where British forces had taken refuge in Nassau Hall, the main building of the College of New Jersey (later Princeton University), then one of the largest buildings on the continent. According to legend, a New York artillery unit, commanded by young Capt. Alexander Hamilton, fired a solid shot that broke through the hall's sturdy front doors and flew through the building. The cannonball smashed into a wall, and it cleanly removed the head from a portrait of King George II. After forty-five minutes, the Battle of Princeton was over, and the Continentals had won yet again.

Assessing his position after this battle, Washington considered moving on to the next British outpost at New Brunswick. However, he decided not to risk another combat situation, knowing that by now Cornwallis's troops must be approaching and that his men could not face the onslaught of this large force. So Washington decided to lead the army into winter quarters in the village of Morristown, an excellent spot for a defensive encampment in the hills west of New York City. There the army could rest, regroup, and make plans for the campaign of 1777. Morristown would be safe from enemy attack, Washington reasoned, and from its hills, he could keep an eye on the main British force based in New York.

THE IMPACT OF THE CROSSING

The "Ten Crucial Days" that began with the Delaware River crossing on December 25 and ended with the American victory in the Battle of Princeton on January 3 had a profound impact on the Colonists' military and political situation. The first victories after a series of costly, embarrassing defeats, the successes in New Jersey provided an extremely important morale boost for both the army and the civilian population. The "glorious day" of the crossing, the subsequent victory at Trenton, and the successes that followed helped preserve the army by encouraging new recruits for the following year. A desperate Washington and his army showed flexibility, risk taking, sacrifice, and innovation, as they endured incredible hardships. The triumphs of the crossing and the battles that followed helped solidify Americans' commitment to gaining independence as a nation.

For Washington, the strategies that were planned during his stay in Pennsylvania enhanced his stature at a time when many doubted his leadership abilities. His aggressiveness, courage, and persistence were recognized as admirable traits, and he became a national hero for his daring in planning and carrying out the New Jersey offensive of 1776–77.

Although the British commander Gen. Sir William Howe minimized the impact of the crossing and the Battles of Trenton and Princeton in his official reports, privately he revealed a loss of confidence and questioned the certainty of his expected victory. For Howe, the events of the "Ten Crucial Days" were evidence that the British would need at least fifteen thousand more soldiers for the planned operations of 1777. "All our hopes were blasted by that unhappy affair at Trenton," complained Lord George Germain, Britain's secretary of state of the American Department.

The Hessians, too, sustained a loss of confidence after losing more than 980 of their best fighters to a motley army of homespun-wearing rebels. Some were now truly frightened of their American foes, who had demonstrated not only a willingness but also an ability to fight. And they marveled that the Americans were so mobile. As one Hessian soldier put it, "The enemy now had wings."

The crossing and the Battles of Trenton and Princeton also had ramifications overseas. The French, not yet formally allied with the rebelling states, now allowed Congress to purchase more weapons and supplies. American contacts with Spain and the Netherlands improved as well, and these nations became sources of loans and supplies.

The crossing, Trenton, and Princeton demonstrated that while the superior British forces could conquer territory and occupy American cities, they then had to garrison these holdings and set up defensive stations. But these outposts were always going to be vulnerable to attack from the mobile American forces. The rebels could cross swollen icy rivers in the bitter cold and blackness of a winter night, endure midnight marches hauling cannons and gear, and defeat the best professional fighting men European monarchs could throw at them. The Revolution was going to go on. Could the British, and their Hessian allies, devise a way to end it?

AFTER THE CROSSING—THE DEVELOPMENT OF TAYLORSVILLE

After the American troops left Bucks County, life in the area of the encampment and the crossing eventually

After the War, Taylorsville thrived as a transportation center for eastern Pennsylvania.

returned to normal. Benjamin Taylor, a Quaker farmer and blacksmith who participated in the militia, purchased the nearby inn and ferry from Samuel McConkey in 1777. Gradually a community known as Taylorsville developed around the tavern. Several generations of Taylors guided its development, among them Benjamin's sons Mahlon Kirkbride Taylor, a lumber merchant, storekeeper, and farm owner, and his brother Bernard.

Taylorsville flourished in the 1830s, when the Delaware Canal opened. As one of the stations along the canal, Taylorsville benefited from the economic success of this new transportation corridor. This waterway, hand dug by Bucks County farmers and imported Irish laborers, paralleled the river and provided the most advanced form of trans-

portation then available in America. Boats carried anthracite from Pennsylvania's coal regions to market in Philadelphia, and manufactured goods from the city on their return trips north. Other materials that floated down the canal were pig iron, lime, grains, and liquor. By the 1850s, these commodities filled three thousand barges that were only ten feet wide but eighty-seven feet long.

When a covered wooden toll bridge replaced the ferry in 1834, more traffic passed through Taylorsville, now nestled between the Delaware River and the canal. Ornamented by two signs painted by noted local Bucks County artist Edward Hicks, the bridge quickly brought additional commerce to the community's general store and post office. The town's assorted artisans, including a tailor, a wheelwright, and

Washington Crossing Historic Park as it appears today.

a shoemaker, also prospered in the mid-nineteenth century.

The enterprising and prolific Taylor clan by now included Samuel, a cabinet-maker who also crafted coffins, and Oliver, the storekeeper. Mahlon's sons Benjamin, a second Oliver, Thomas, and Augustus also worked at the store by midcentury. By now the community had grown large enough to require its own school, and a church was built for a Methodist congregation on land donated by William Taylor.

Although the canal's relative importance declined after the Civil War (1861–65), when America turned to railroads for faster and more regular transportation, the waterway stayed in business until the 1930s. In 1940, the sixty-mile canal and its towpath were designated the Delaware Canal State Park, and in 1988, the facility was included in the Delaware and Lehigh National Heritage Corridor.

CREATION OF THE PARK

As the nineteenth century drew to a close, Americans began to acknowledge historic events and sites with greater interest. The United States Centennial Exposition, held in Philadelphia's Fairmount Park in 1876, played a large role in fostering a new appreciation of the nation's past. Often, local groups led the way in these efforts. This was the case in Taylorsville, where in 1895 the Bucks County Historical Society placed a stone marker at the spot from which Washington's army launched its Christmas night 1776 crossing of the Delaware River.

In 1917, urged on by a concerted effort of the Bucks County Historical Society, the Daughters of the American Revolution, the Patriotic Order of the Sons of America, and the Historical Society of Pennsylvania, the commonwealth created the Washington Crossing Park Commission. The park was established that year, and in 1918, the name of the Taylorsville post office was changed to Washington Crossing.

Today the five-hundred-plus-acre park hosts thousands of visitors every year, from local schoolchildren to visitors from around the world, who come to see the point from which a battered and dispirited American army launched a counterattack that reversed its long losing streak, preserving its will to fight and maintaining the revolutionary spirit that would lead to independence for the United States.

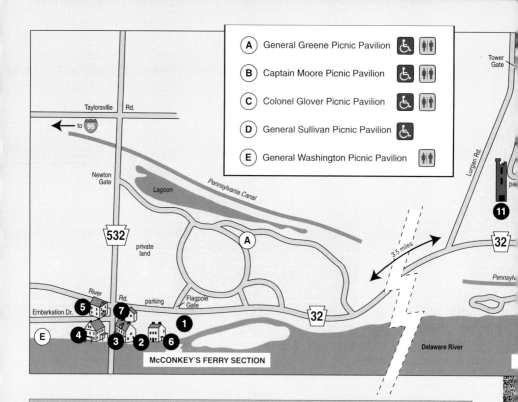

A	General Greene Picnic Pavilion ♿ 🚻
B	Captain Moore Picnic Pavilion ♿ 🚻
C	Colonel Glover Picnic Pavilion ♿ 🚻
D	General Sullivan Picnic Pavilion ♿
E	General Washington Picnic Pavilion 🚻

Tower Gate

Taylorsville Rd.

to 95

Newton Gate

Pennsylvania Canal

Lagoon

Lurgan Rd.

11

532

private land

A

32

3.5 miles

Pennsylv

River Rd.

parking

Flagpole Gate

5 7

Embarkation Dr.

E 4 3 2 6 1

32

Delaware River

McCONKEY'S FERRY SECTION

SITE LEGEND

McCONKEY FERRY SECTION

1 Visitor Center

2 Durham Boat Barn

3 McConkey Ferry Inn

4 Mahlon K. Taylor House

5 Taylorsville Store

6 Hibbs House

7 Frye House and Blacksmith Shop

THOMPSON'S MILL SECTION

8 Thompson-Neely House

9 Thompson-Neely Gristmill

10 Bowman's Hill Wildflower Preserve

11 Bowman's Hill Tower

12 Soldiers' Graves

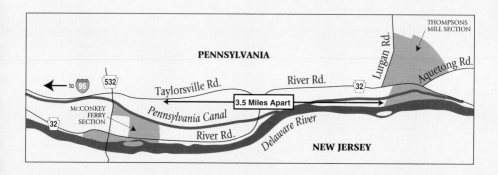

THOMPSONS MILL SECTION

PENNSYLVANIA

Lurgan Rd.

Aquetong Rd.

to 95 532

Taylorsville Rd.

River Rd.

32

McCONKEY FERRY SECTION

32

Pennsylvania Canal

3.5 Miles Apart

River Rd.

Delaware River

NEW JERSEY

Visiting the Site

Washington Crossing Historic Park consists of two sections that are approximately 4.5 miles apart. **The McConkey Ferry Section,** which includes the actual crossing site, is located at the intersection of Pennsylvania Routes 32 and 532. The Visitor Center is also located in this section.

Bowman's Hill

parking

Creek

10

B

Aquetong Rd.

West Gate

Thompson-Neely Gate

parking

River Rd.

C

D

N'S MILL SECTION

1 VISITOR CENTER

The Visitor Center houses the admissions desk, museum shop, administrative offices, keystone-shaped auditorium, and restrooms. Exhibits, a brief orientation video, and an exact replica of Emanuel Leutze's painting *Washington Crossing the Delaware* introduce the park. Guided tours of the McConkey Ferry Section begin here.

② DURHAM BOAT BARN

In the eighteenth century, Durham boats, originally designed by Robert Durham of the Durham Iron Works, were used to carry iron ore and other trade products down the Delaware River to processing sites and markets in Philadelphia. Durham boats could carry twenty tons of cargo and still have a shallow draft, so they were ideally suited for a river that could be very shallow at times, such as the Delaware. After the Revolution, Durham boats carried cargo up and down the Delaware for more than half a century, but their use decreased when the Delaware Canal was opened in the 1830s; however, Durhams were used up to the 1860s.

Depending on the river, the boats could be rowed with oars eighteen feet long or the crewmen could use set poles to move the boats along. They could also be sailed. A movable steering oar called a sweep allowed these boats to be guided from either bow or stern.

Durham boats ranged from forty to sixty feet long and were eight feet wide. The replicas in this twentieth-century building are approximately forty feet long. The park's first two replica Durham boats were built in 1965 and 1976 in Point Pleasant, New Jersey, by the Johnson Brothers Boat Works. Boatbuilder Paul Rollins of York, Maine, constructed the other reproductions in 1996 and 1997.

Durham boats were among those that transported Washington's troops across the icy Delaware on Christmas 1776. When Washington's crossing is reenacted each year on Christmas Day, these flat-bottomed boats carry the participants across to the New Jersey side of the river. The steel bridge that is so prominent today was constructed in 1904 and was not available to Washington and his men.

③ MCCONKEY FERRY INN

The Baker family built the first ferry on this site, one of many Delaware River ferry sites in Bucks County. The Bakers sold it to Samuel McConkey, who was the owner in 1776. The inn was built in several stages; the west side, the one farthest from the river, was built around 1750. The building represents a typical country inn or tavern of the Revolutionary era and suggests the variety of amenities that would have been available to the traveler at that time.

During the Continental army's stay in Bucks County in December 1776, the inn and the nearby ferry launch site were closely guarded by the troops. Tradition has it that Washington ate a meal at the McConkey Ferry Inn, where on the evening of the crossing, he wrote to Colonel Cadwalader, "I am determined as the night is favorable . . ."

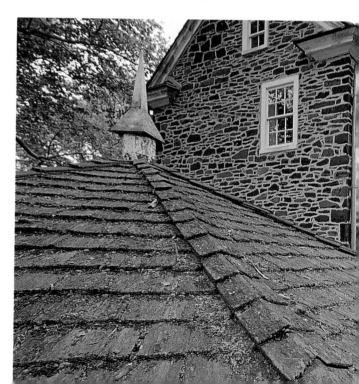

4 MAHLON K. TAYLOR HOUSE

Born in 1791, Mahlon K. Taylor became the wealthiest and most influential member of the Taylor family. He was a fixture of Taylorsville's commercial success until his death in 1870.

The stately home illustrates Taylor's successful career as a merchant and entrepreneur. The house is a fine example of the degree to which the fashions and refinement of upper-class Philadelphians were beginning to influence rural Pennsylvania. Built in 1816, the house epitomized Taylor's success.

5 **TAYLORSVILLE STORE**

Many nineteenth-century country villages and towns had general stores that sold a wide array of merchandise. A small community typically had only one general store, which housed the post office, displayed notices, and circulated information.

Mahlon Taylor opened the Taylorsville Store about 1824, shortly before the canal was constructed, and he used it as the base of his business operations for almost forty years. The restored building once again serves as a general store, offering a wide

array of items related to the park's history among its extensive inventory. The store's cellar snack bar provides tasty luncheon items, ice cream, and cold drinks to make a summer visit to the site more pleasant.

6 **HIBBS HOUSE**

This simple house, built in 1828, was one of many Mahlon Taylor had constructed to lease to local artisans. It served as the home and workshop of a shoemaker, then a wheelwright, and finally a carpenter, Abdon Hibbs. The structure is a typical two-room over two-room stone tenant house, used to house a worker and his family, as well as an apprentice.

7 FRYE HOUSE AND BLACKSMITH SHOP

Bernard Taylor built the Frye House in 1828 as a tenant property. It housed Taylorsville's blacksmith and his family, as well as an apprentice. The blacksmith was an indispensable con-tributor to American life. With strength and skill, he fashioned iron tools and implements that were essential to work and to family life in the preindustrial era. Taylorsville's original Blacksmith Shop was constructed about 1830. The current shop was built in 1990. Living-history demonstrations are conducted here during special events throughout the year.

The **Thompson's Mill Section** of the park is located on Pennsylvania Route 32, also known as River Road, 4.5 miles north of the McConkey Ferry Section. Parking is available at several locations in this area.

❸ THOMPSON-NEELY HOUSE

The Thompson-Neely House is a fine example of Bucks County vernacular architecture. Early Scots-Irish settler John Pidcock, who farmed and traded with the Native Americans, settled on this site in 1702. In the 1730s, the Simpson family constructed the original section of this house. In 1757, owners Robert and Hannah Thompson built a two-story addition on the west end (away from the river). Shortly thereafter, they added a second story above the old first section, creating a continuous roofline. A miller, Robert Thompson became one of the wealthiest landowners in the area by the time of the Revolution.

During the Continental Army's stay in Bucks County, the Thompson House served as an army hospital. A young officer from Virginia named James Monroe, who was seriously injured during the First

Battle of Trenton convalesced here. In 1817, he became the fifth president of the United States. Wounded with Monroe was William Washington, a distant cousin of the commander in chief. He too recovered at this location.

In 1766, Elizabeth Thompson, daughter of Robert and Hannah, married an Irish immigrant named William Neely, who continued to farm and run the mill on the property. The Neelys enlarged the house once again by constructing the two-story east wing in 1788. Taller ceilings gave the newest portion a higher roofline than the existing structure, and the elements of classical design

reflect the changing tastes in American architecture.

Once the centerpiece of a working farm and milling complex, the Thompson-Neely House was surrounded by numerous outbuildings such as the restored barn, smokehouse, and privy seen today.

9 THOMPSON-NEELY GRISTMILL

Water-powered mills were common in southeastern Pennsylvania well into the nineteenth century, before steam engines and other newer technologies began to replace them. William Neely built this gristmill in the 1830s. It was used to grind grain from nearby farms, such as corn and wheat, into meal or flour for the use of the farmer and his family or to be sold to a broader regional market.

Although they appear primitive by today's standards, water-powered mills represented the accomplishments of skilled designers and builders who had a basic understanding of hydraulics and the mathematics of gear ratios, drive shafts, and other components. Smooth operation of the mill required many fine adjustments to the interconnected system made of wood, metal, leather, and stone parts. The miller or one of his workers was responsible

45

for maintaining and repairing the complex machinery.

Historical records indicate that an earlier mill, possibly constructed during the previous century, was located on this property about one hundred yards farther down Pidcock Creek from the existing mill. The older mill may have sheltered American soldiers during the Bucks County encampment in 1776 and may have provided flour to feed the troops.

BOWMAN'S HILL WILDFLOWER PRESERVE

Following Pidcock Creek upstream from the gristmill, visitors find a charming spot where many of Pennsylvania's native plants are preserved and exhibited. Developed in 1934, Bowman's Hill Wildflower Preserve was the first of its kind in the United States. The Bowman's Hill Wildflower Preserve Association, a local botanical society that operates under a special agreement with the Pennsylvania Historical and Museum Commission, has developed walking trails that meander through the preserve and presents public programs. The Headquarters building has indoor exhibits and a gift shop with merchandise relating to wild plants and flowers of Pennsylvania.

BOWMAN'S HILL TOWER

Overlooking the Delaware River, Bowman's Hill supports another unique feature: a 125-foot, medieval-looking stone tower, which was completed in 1931, at the hill's summit. Today an elevator takes visitors to the tower's observation platform. The view from the top is spectacular, presenting miles of Bucks County landscape and a peek into neighboring New Jersey as well. The tower is open on a seasonal basis. An access road leads to the adjacent parking area.

SOLDIERS' GRAVES

From the parking area at the Thompson-Neely House, it is a short walk across the Delaware Canal to the memorial cemetery where about forty Continental soldiers who died during the December 1776 encampment in Bucks County are buried. Although no Americans were killed during the crossing and the First Battle of Trenton, others did succumb to exposure, disease, or previous injuries.

James Moore, a twenty-six-year-old artillery captain from

a New York regiment, is the only veteran buried in this plot whose identity is assumed. The others are unknown.

For information on hours, tours, programs, and activities at Washington Crossing Historic Park, visit **www.phmc.state.pa.us** or call **215-493-4076.**

Further Reading

Barnes, Ian. *The Historical Atlas of the American Revolution*. New York: Routledge, 2000.

Blanco, Richard L., ed. *The American Revolution 1775–1783: An Encyclopedia*. 2 vols. New York and London: Garland Publishing, 1993.

Dwyer, William M. *The Day Is Ours: November 1776–January 1777: An Inside View of the Battles of Trenton and Princeton*. New York: Viking Press, 1983.

Fischer, David Hackett. *Washington's Crossing*. New York: Oxford University Press, 2004.

Harvey, Robert. *"A Few Bloody Noses": The Realities and Mythologies of the American Revolution*. London: John Murray, 2001.

Ketchum, Richard M. *The Winter Soldiers: The Battles for Trenton and Princeton*. 1973; reprint, New York: Henry Holt and Company, 1999.

Lefkowitz, Arthur S. *The Long Retreat: The Calamitous American Defense of New Jersey, 1776*. New Brunswick, N.J.: Rutgers University Press, 1998.

Mackesy, Piers. *The War for America, 1775–1783*. Lincoln, Neb.: University of Nebraska Press, 1993.

Raphael, Ray. *A People's History of the American Revolution: How Common People Shaped the Fight for Independence*. New York: HarperCollins, 2002.

Stryker, William. *The Battles of Trenton and Princeton*. 1898; reprint, Trenton, N.J.: Old Barracks Museum, 2001.

Wolf, Stephanie Grauman. *As Various as Their Land: The Everyday Lives of Eighteenth-Century Americans*. New York: HarperPerennial, 1993.

Also Available

Anthracite Heritage Museum
and Scranton Iron Furnaces

Brandywine Battlefield Park

Bushy Run Battlefield

Conrad Weiser Homestead

Cornwall Iron Furnace

Daniel Boone Homestead

Drake Well Museum and Park

Eckley Miners' Village

Ephrata Cloister

Erie Maritime Museum and
U.S. Brig Niagara

Fort Pitt Museum

Graeme Park

Hope Lodge and Mather Mill

Joseph Priestley House

Landis Valley Museum

Old Economy Village

Pennsbury Manor

Railroad Museum
of Pennsylvania

All titles are $10, plus shipping,
from Stackpole Books, 800-732-3669, www.stackpolebooks.com, or
The Pennsylvania Historical and Museum Commission, 800-747-7790,
www.phmc.state.pa.us